AI for All: Transformative Artificial Intelligence

ISBN: 978-1-987931-19-8

Dedication

To the young people and future generations around the world, You are the torchbearers of Transformative Artificial Intelligence, making this world a better place.

May your curiosity, creativity, and passion drive the innovations that will shape our future. Your dedication and vision will light the path towards a brighter, more inclusive, and sustainable world.

To all the pioneers and visionaries in the field of Artificial Intelligence, whose relentless pursuit of knowledge and innovation continues to inspire.

And to every reader, may this book ignite your curiosity and passion for the transformative power of AI.

AI for All: Transformative Artificial Intelligence

AI for All

Transformative Artificial

Intelligence, with benefits and risks

Dr. Farzana Chohan

Table of Contents

AI for All: Transformative Artificial Intelligence

AI for All: Transformative Artificial Intelligence

Introduction

Artificial Intelligence (AI) and Its Rapid Development

Artificial Intelligence (AI) has evolved from a theoretical concept to a transformative force in just a few decades. The journey began in the mid-20th century with pioneers like Alan Turing, who laid the groundwork for machine learning and computational theory. Since then, AI has made significant strides, from the development of expert systems in the 1980s to the advent of deep learning and neural networks in the 21st century. Today, AI encompasses a wide range of technologies, including natural language processing, computer vision, and robotics, all of which are advancing at an unprecedented pace.

The Significance of AI in Modern Society

AI's impact on modern society is profound and multifaceted. In healthcare, AI algorithms are revolutionizing diagnostics and personalized medicine, enabling early detection of diseases and tailored treatment plans. In transportation, autonomous vehicles promise to reduce accidents and improve traffic management. The education sector is also benefiting from AI, with personalized learning platforms that adapt to individual student needs. Moreover, AI is playing a crucial role in environmental conservation, from climate modeling to wildlife protection.

However, the rapid development of AI also brings challenges. Ethical concerns, such as bias in AI algorithms and privacy issues, are becoming increasingly prominent. The economic impact of AI, including job displacement and income inequality, is a topic of intense debate. Additionally, the security risks associated with AI, such as its use in cyber warfare and autonomous weapons, pose significant threats. Despite these challenges, the potential benefits of AI are immense, and its continued development holds the promise of a better future for humanity.

So where is AI Balance?

It is important for everyone to navigate the benefits and risks of Artificial Intelligence

Artificial Intelligence (AI) has become an integral part of our lives, influencing various sectors and transforming the way we live and work. However, the rapid development and integration of AI also bring significant challenges and risks. Striking a balance between harnessing the benefits of AI and mitigating its potential drawbacks is crucial for creating a future where AI serves as a force for good.

The Promises of AI

AI holds immense potential to revolutionize industries and improve the quality of life. In healthcare, AI algorithms can analyze vast amounts of medical data to provide accurate and timely diagnoses, leading to better patient outcomes. Personalized medicine, powered by AI, tailors treatment plans to individual patients, enhancing the effectiveness of treatments and reducing adverse reactions. In transportation, autonomous vehicles promise to reduce traffic accidents and improve traffic management, making travel safer and more efficient. AI-powered personalized learning platforms in education adapt to individual student needs, fostering a more effective and inclusive learning environment. Additionally, AI plays a crucial role in environmental conservation, aiding in climate modeling and wildlife protection.

The Perils of AI

Despite its promises, AI also presents significant challenges and risks. Ethical concerns, such as bias in AI algorithms and privacy issues, are becoming increasingly prominent. AI systems trained on biased datasets can perpetuate and amplify existing biases, leading to unfair treatment of certain groups. Privacy violations are another major concern, as AI systems often require vast amounts of personal data to function effectively. The economic impact of AI, including job displacement and income inequality, is a topic of intense debate. As AI automates routine tasks, many jobs are at risk of being replaced, leading to increased unemployment and economic disparities. Security risks, such as the use of AI in cyber warfare and autonomous weapons, pose significant threats to national security and public trust8. Social implications, including the erosion of human touch in interactions and increased dependency on technology, also need to be carefully considered9.

Navigating the AI Landscape

To navigate the benefits and risks of AI, a multifaceted approach is required. Ethical AI development practices, robust policies and regulations, and widespread education and public engagement are essential. Incorporating fairness, accountability, and transparency into AI systems is crucial to ensure that they do not perpetuate biases or discrimination0. Governments and regulatory bodies play a vital role in setting standards for data privacy, security, and ethical AI development. Education and public awareness are

AI for All: Transformative Artificial Intelligence

key to fostering a more informed and engaged society, capable of making informed decisions about AI's future.

By taking these steps, we can harness the positive potential of AI while addressing its challenges. Striking a balance between the benefits and risks of AI is essential for creating a future where AI serves as a force for good, driving progress and improving the quality of life for all.

Chapter1: The Rise of AI

Historical Background of AI Development

The concept of artificial intelligence dates back to ancient times, with myths and stories about artificial beings endowed with intelligence. However, the formal development of AI began in the mid-20th century. In 1950, Alan Turing, a British mathematician and logician, proposed the idea of a machine that could simulate any human intelligence task, known as the Turing Test. This marked the beginning of AI as a field of study.

In 1956, the term "artificial intelligence" was coined at the Dartmouth Conference, where researchers gathered to discuss the potential of creating machines that could think and learn like humans. This conference is often considered the birth of AI as an academic discipline. Early AI research focused on symbolic AI, which involved programming computers to manipulate symbols and solve problems using logical rules.

Key Milestones and Breakthroughs in AI Technology

Over the decades, AI has achieved several significant milestones. In the 1960s and 1970s, researchers developed expert systems, which were designed to mimic the decision-making abilities of human experts in specific domains. One of the most famous expert systems was MYCIN, developed in the 1970s to diagnose bacterial infections and recommend treatments.

The 1980s saw the rise of machine learning, a subfield of AI that focuses on developing algorithms that allow computers to learn from data. This period also witnessed the development of neural networks, inspired by the structure and function of the human brain. However, due to limited computational power and data, progress in neural networks was slow.

The 21st century brought significant advancements in AI, particularly with the advent of deep learning. **Deep learning involves training large neural networks with multiple layers, enabling them to learn complex**

patterns from vast amounts of data. Breakthroughs in deep learning have led to remarkable achievements in various fields, such as image and speech recognition, natural language processing, and autonomous systems.

Introduction to Major AI Technologies

AI encompasses a wide range of technologies, each with its unique capabilities and applications. Some of the major AI technologies include:

- **Machine Learning**: *A subset of AI that focuses on developing algorithms that enable computers to learn from and make predictions based on data. Machine learning is used in various applications, such as recommendation systems, fraud detection, and predictive analytics.*

- **Neural Networks**: Computational models inspired by the human brain, consisting of interconnected nodes (neurons) that process information. Neural networks are the foundation of deep learning and are used in tasks such as image and speech recognition.

- **Natural Language Processing (NLP)**: *A field of AI that focuses on enabling computers to understand, interpret, and generate human language. NLP is used in applications such as chatbots, language translation, and sentiment analysis.*

- **Computer Vision**: *A field of AI that enables computers to interpret and understand visual information from the world. Computer vision is used in applications such as facial recognition, object detection, and autonomous vehicles.*

- **Robotics**: The integration of AI with robotics to create intelligent machines that can perform tasks autonomously. AI-powered robots are used in various industries, including manufacturing, healthcare, and logistics.

These technologies are advancing rapidly, driving the AI revolution and transforming various aspects of our lives.

Chapter 2: The Benefits of AI

Enhancements in Healthcare

Artificial Intelligence is revolutionizing the healthcare industry in numerous ways. AI algorithms are being used to analyze medical data and assist in diagnostics, leading to more accurate and timely diagnoses. For instance, AI can analyze medical images such as X-rays, MRIs, and CT scans to detect abnormalities that might be missed by the human eye. This has proven particularly useful in early detection of diseases like cancer, where early intervention can significantly improve patient outcomes.

Personalized medicine is another area where AI is making a significant impact. By analyzing a patient's genetic information, lifestyle, and medical history, AI can help tailor treatment plans that are specifically designed for the individual. This approach not only improves the effectiveness of treatments but also reduces the risk of adverse reactions.

Improvements in Transportation

The transportation sector is experiencing a transformation thanks to AI. Autonomous vehicles, powered by AI, are being developed to navigate roads, recognize traffic signals, and avoid obstacles without human intervention. These self-driving cars have the potential to reduce traffic accidents caused by human error, thereby saving lives and reducing injuries.

AI is also being used to improve traffic management. By analyzing data from various sources such as traffic cameras, sensors, and GPS devices, AI systems can optimize traffic flow, reduce congestion, and minimize travel time. This not only enhances the efficiency of transportation networks but also reduces fuel consumption and emissions, contributing to a cleaner environment.

Advancements in Education

In the field of education, AI is enabling personalized learning experiences for students. AI-powered platforms can assess a student's strengths and weaknesses and then adapt the curriculum to meet their individual needs. This personalized approach helps students learn at their own pace and ensures that they receive the support they need to succeed.

AI tutors are another innovation in education. These virtual tutors can provide students with instant feedback, answer their questions, and offer additional resources to help them understand complex concepts. This not only enhances the learning experience but also allows teachers to focus on more critical aspects of education, such as fostering creativity and critical thinking skills.

AI in Environmental Conservation

AI is playing a crucial role in environmental conservation efforts. Climate modeling is one area where AI is making a significant impact. By analyzing vast amounts of data, AI can help scientists predict climate patterns, understand the effects of climate change, and develop strategies to mitigate its impact.

AI for All: Transformative Artificial Intelligence

Wildlife protection is another area where AI is proving beneficial. AI-powered drones and cameras are being used to monitor wildlife populations, track animal movements, and detect illegal activities such as poaching. This technology enables conservationists to gather valuable data and take timely action to protect endangered species.

These are just a few examples of how AI is positively impacting various sectors. The potential benefits of AI are immense, and its continued development holds the promise of a better future for humanity.

Let's briefly read some more examples of real-world AI applications.

Examples of Artificial Intelligence (AI), its rapid development and usage in our modern world

The Rise of DeepMind's AlphaGo

One of the most remarkable examples of AI's rapid development is the story of DeepMind's AlphaGo. In 2016, AlphaGo, an AI program developed by DeepMind, made headlines by defeating Lee Sedol, one of the world's top Go players. Go is an ancient board game known for its complexity and the vast number of possible moves. AlphaGo's victory was a significant milestone in AI development, showcasing the power of deep learning and neural networks. This achievement demonstrated that AI could master complex tasks that were previously thought to be the exclusive domain of human intelligence1.

AI in Healthcare - IBM Watson

IBM Watson is a prime example of how AI is transforming healthcare. Watson, an AI system developed by IBM, has been used to assist doctors in diagnosing and treating patients. In one notable case, Watson analyzed a patient's medical records and identified a rare form of leukemia that had been missed by human doctors. By sifting through vast amounts of medical literature and patient data, Watson was able to provide a diagnosis and recommend a personalized treatment plan. This example highlights the potential of AI to enhance medical diagnostics and improve patient outcomes.

AI in Transportation - Waymo's Autonomous Vehicles

Waymo, a subsidiary of Alphabet Inc., is at the forefront of developing autonomous vehicles. Waymo's self-driving cars have been tested extensively on public roads and have accumulated millions of miles of driving experience. In

2020, Waymo launched a fully autonomous ride-hailing service in Phoenix, Arizona, allowing passengers to travel without a human driver. This development marks a significant step towards the widespread adoption of autonomous vehicles, which have the potential to reduce traffic accidents, improve traffic flow, and provide greater mobility for people with disabilities.

AI in Education - Duolingo

Duolingo, a popular language-learning app, leverages AI to provide personalized learning experiences for its users. The app uses machine learning algorithms to adapt lessons based on the user's progress and performance. For example, if a user struggles with a particular concept, Duolingo will provide additional practice and reinforcement. This personalized approach helps users learn more effectively and at their own pace. Duolingo's success demonstrates how AI can enhance education by tailoring learning experiences to individual needs.

AI in Environmental Conservation - Wildlife

Protection with AI-Powered Drones

AI-powered drones are being used to monitor and protect wildlife in various parts of the world. In Africa, for example, drones equipped with AI algorithms are used to track and monitor endangered species such as elephants and rhinos. These drones can detect poachers and alert authorities in real-time, helping to prevent illegal activities and protect wildlife. This innovative use of AI technology is making a significant impact on conservation efforts and helping to preserve biodiversity.

These real-life stories illustrate the rapid development of AI and its profound impact on various aspects of modern society. From healthcare and transportation to education and environmental conservation, AI is transforming industries and improving the quality of life for people around the world.

Chapter 3: The Risks of AI

Ethical Concerns

One of the most pressing ethical concerns surrounding AI is bias in algorithms. AI systems are trained on large datasets, and if these datasets contain biased information, the AI can perpetuate and even amplify these biases. This can lead to unfair treatment of certain groups of people, particularly in areas like hiring, lending, and law enforcement. For example, facial recognition technology has been shown to have higher error rates for people with darker skin tones, leading to potential misidentification and discrimination.

Privacy issues are another significant ethical concern. AI systems often require vast amounts of data to function effectively, and this data can include sensitive personal information. There is a risk that this data could be misused or inadequately protected, leading to breaches of privacy. Additionally, the use of AI in surveillance can lead to a loss of anonymity and increased monitoring of individuals' activities, raising concerns about the erosion of civil liberties.

Economic Impact

The economic impact of AI is a topic of intense debate. On one hand, AI has the potential to drive economic growth by increasing productivity and creating new industries. On the other hand, it also poses a threat to jobs, particularly those that involve routine and repetitive tasks. As AI systems become more capable, there is a risk that many jobs could be automated, leading to job displacement and increased unemployment.

Income inequality is another economic concern associated with AI. The benefits of AI are often concentrated among a small group of people, such as tech companies and highly skilled workers, while others may be left behind. This can exacerbate existing economic disparities and create a divide between those who can take advantage of AI and those who cannot.

Security Risks

AI also presents significant security risks. One of the most concerning is the potential use of AI in cyber warfare. AI can be used to develop sophisticated cyberattacks that are difficult to detect and defend against. For example, AI-powered malware can adapt to security measures and evade detection, making it a potent tool for cybercriminals.

Autonomous weapons are another security risk associated with AI. These weapons can operate without human intervention, making decisions about targeting and engagement on their own. This raises ethical and practical concerns about the potential for unintended consequences and the loss of human control over lethal force.

Social Implications

This rapid development of AI also has social implications. One concern is the increasing dependency on technology. As AI systems become more integrated into our daily lives, there is a risk that people may become overly reliant on them, leading to a loss of critical thinking and problem-solving skills.

Another social implication is the potential loss of human touch. AI systems, such as chatbots and virtual assistants, are increasingly being used in customer service and other interactions. While these systems can be efficient, they lack the empathy and understanding that human interactions provide. This can lead to a sense of isolation and a decrease in the quality of human relationships.

These are some of the not-so-good aspects of AI that need to be carefully considered and addressed as we continue to develop and integrate AI technologies into our society.

Ethical Concerns

Let's review the lessons learned about the risks from real world AI applications.

Bias in AI Algorithms - COMPAS

One of the most well-known examples of bias in AI algorithms is the COMPAS (Correctional Offender Management Profiling for Alternative Sanctions) system used in the United States to assess the likelihood of a defendant reoffending. A ProPublica investigation in 2016 revealed that COMPAS was biased against African Americans, who were more likely to be incorrectly classified as high-risk compared to white defendants. This bias in the algorithm led to unfair treatment and raised significant ethical concerns about the use of AI in the criminal justice system.

Privacy Issues - Cambridge Analytica

The Cambridge Analytica scandal is a prime example of privacy issues associated with AI. In 2018, it was revealed that Cambridge Analytica had harvested the personal data of millions of Facebook users without their consent and used this data to influence political campaigns. The scandal highlighted the potential for AI to misuse personal data and the need for robust data protection measures to safeguard privacy.

Economic Impact

Job Displacement - Automation in Manufacturing

The rise of AI and automation has led to significant job displacement in various industries, particularly in manufacturing. For example, the introduction of AI-powered robots in automotive manufacturing has resulted in the loss of many assembly line jobs. While automation has increased efficiency and productivity, it has also left many workers unemployed and struggling to find new employment opportunities.

Income Inequality - Tech Industry

The benefits of AI are often concentrated among a small group of people, such as tech companies and highly skilled workers, while others may be left behind. This has exacerbated existing economic disparities and created a divide between those who can take advantage of AI and those who cannot. For instance, tech giants like Google and Amazon have seen significant financial gains from AI advancements, while many workers in traditional industries face job insecurity and stagnant wages.

Security Risks

AI in Cyber Warfare - Deepfake Technology

Deepfake technology, which uses AI to create realistic but fake videos and audio recordings, poses significant security risks. In 2019, a deepfake video of Facebook CEO Mark Zuckerberg went viral, showing him making statements he never actually made. This technology can be used to spread misinformation, manipulate public opinion, and even blackmail individuals, highlighting the potential dangers of AI in cyber warfare.

Autonomous Weapons - Lethal Autonomous Weapons Systems (LAWS)

The development of lethal autonomous weapons systems (LAWS) has raised ethical and security concerns. These weapons can operate without human intervention, making decisions about targeting and engagement on their own. The potential for unintended consequences and the loss of human control over lethal force has led to calls for international regulations to prevent the proliferation of autonomous weapons.

Social Implications

Dependency on Technology - AI Assistants

The increasing dependency on AI assistants like Amazon's Alexa and Google Assistant has raised concerns about the loss of critical thinking and problem-solving skills. As people rely more on these AI systems for everyday tasks, there is a risk that they may become overly reliant on technology, leading to a decline in cognitive abilities and self-sufficiency7.

Loss of Human Touch - AI in Customer Service

AI systems, such as chatbots and virtual assistants, are increasingly being used in customer service. While these systems can be efficient, they lack the empathy and understanding that human interactions provide. This can lead to a sense of isolation and a decrease in the quality of human relationships. For example, customers may feel frustrated and disconnected when dealing with an AI chatbot that cannot fully understand their concerns.

These real-life stories illustrate the ethical concerns, economic impacts, security risks, and social implications associated with AI. It is essential to address these challenges as we continue to develop and integrate AI technologies into our society.

Chapter 4: Balancing the Benefits

and Risks

Strategies for Ethical AI Development

Developing AI ethically is crucial to ensure that its benefits are maximized while minimizing potential harms. One key strategy is to incorporate fairness, accountability, and transparency into AI systems. This involves designing algorithms that are free from bias and ensuring that AI decisions can be explained and justified. Regular audits and assessments can help identify and mitigate any biases or unintended consequences.

Another important strategy is to involve diverse stakeholders in the AI development process. This includes not only engineers and data scientists but also ethicists, sociologists, and representatives from affected communities. By considering a wide range of perspectives, developers can create AI systems that are more inclusive and equitable.

Policies and Regulations to Ensure Responsible AI Use

Governments and regulatory bodies play a vital role in ensuring the responsible use of AI. Policies and regulations can set standards for data privacy, security, and ethical AI development. For example, the General Data Protection Regulation (GDPR) in the European Union provides guidelines for data protection and privacy, which are essential for AI systems that rely on large datasets.

Regulations can also address the potential economic impacts of AI, such as job displacement. Policies that promote reskilling and upskilling of workers can help mitigate the negative effects of automation. Additionally, regulations can ensure that AI is used responsibly in critical areas such as healthcare, finance, and law enforcement, where the stakes are particularly high.

Role of Education and Public Awareness in

Shaping AI's Future

Education and public awareness are key to shaping the future of AI. By educating the public about AI and its implications, we can foster a more informed and engaged society. This includes integrating AI education into school curricula, offering training programs for professionals, and providing resources for lifelong learning.

Public awareness campaigns can also help demystify AI and address common misconceptions. By highlighting both the benefits and risks of AI, these campaigns can encourage a balanced and nuanced understanding of the technology. Engaging the public in discussions about AI ethics and governance can also help build trust and ensure that AI development aligns with societal values.

Balancing the benefits and risks of AI requires a multifaceted approach that includes ethical development practices, robust policies and regulations, and widespread education and public engagement. By taking these steps, we can harness the power of AI to create a better future for all.

Strategies for Ethical AI Development

Just like any new thing we adept in life Let's briefly read some more examples of real-world AI applications.

Google's AI Principles

In 2018, Google published a set of AI principles to guide the ethical development and use of AI technologies. These principles include commitments to avoid creating or reinforcing unfair bias, ensuring AI systems are accountable to people, and incorporating privacy design principles. One notable example of these principles in action is Google's decision to discontinue its involvement in Project Maven, a U.S. Department of Defense initiative that aimed to use AI for analyzing drone footage. Google employees raised ethical concerns about the potential use of AI in warfare, leading the company to prioritize ethical considerations over potential profits12.

Policies and Regulations to Ensure Responsible AI Use

The General Data Protection Regulation (GDPR)

The General Data Protection Regulation (GDPR) in the European Union is a landmark policy that sets standards for data protection and privacy. Implemented in 2018, GDPR provides guidelines for how personal data should be collected, stored, and processed, ensuring that individuals have control over their data. Companies that fail to comply with GDPR can face significant fines. This regulation has had a profound impact on how AI systems handle personal data, promoting transparency and accountability in AI development3.

Role of Education and Public Awareness in Shaping AI's Future

Finland's AI Education Initiative

In 2018, Finland launched an initiative called "Elements of AI," an online course designed to educate the public about artificial intelligence. The course covers the basics of AI, its applications, and its implications for society. It has been translated into multiple languages and made available for free to people around the world. This initiative aims to demystify AI, promote public understanding, and encourage informed discussions about the technology's future. By educating the public, Finland is fostering a more informed and engaged society that can actively participate in shaping the future of AI.

These real-life stories illustrate how ethical AI development, robust policies and regulations, and education and public awareness can help balance the

AI for All: Transformative Artificial Intelligence

benefits and risks of AI. By taking these steps, we can harness the power of AI to create a better future for all.

Chapter 5: Utopian, Dystopian and Mediocre - Three AI world scenarios

Artificial Intelligence (AI) has the potential to shape the future of our world in profound ways. Depending on how it is developed, implemented, and regulated, AI can lead to vastly different outcomes for society. In this section, we explore three distinct scenarios of 1. AI: a utopian AI world, 2. a mediocre AI world, and 3. a dystopian AI world. Each scenario presents a unique vision of the future, highlighting the promises, challenges, and risks associated with AI.

Through these three scenarios, we aim to provide a comprehensive exploration of the potential futures shaped by AI. By understanding the promises, challenges, and risks associated with AI, we can make informed decisions and take proactive steps to ensure that AI serves as a force for good in our society.

Utopian AI World

In the utopian AI world, AI has reached its full potential, creating a harmonious and prosperous society. AI technologies are seamlessly integrated into every aspect of life, enhancing human well-being and fostering a sustainable and equitable world. Healthcare is revolutionized with personalized medicine and advanced diagnostics, transportation is safe and efficient with autonomous vehicles, education is personalized and accessible to all, and environmental conservation efforts are bolstered by AI-driven solutions. Ethical considerations and robust regulations ensure that AI is developed and used responsibly, promoting fairness, transparency, and accountability. In this scenario, AI serves as a force for good, driving progress and improving the quality of life for all.

Imagine a Utopian AI world, where the best positive potential of AI has become a reality

Imagine a world where artificial intelligence (AI) has reached its full potential, creating a utopian society where technology seamlessly integrates with every aspect of life, enhancing human well-being and fostering a harmonious existence. In this utopian AI world, the positive potential of AI is harnessed to its fullest, transforming various sectors and improving the quality of life for all.

Healthcare

In this utopian world, healthcare is revolutionized by AI. Advanced AI algorithms analyze vast amounts of medical data to provide accurate and timely diagnoses, often before symptoms even appear. Personalized medicine becomes the norm, with AI systems tailoring treatment plans to everyone's genetic makeup, lifestyle, and medical history. AI-powered robotic surgeons perform complex surgeries with precision, reducing recovery times and improving outcomes. Preventive healthcare is also enhanced, with AI monitoring individuals' health in real-time and providing personalized recommendations to maintain optimal well-being.

Transportation

Transportation is transformed by AI, making travel safer, more efficient, and environmentally friendly. Autonomous vehicles dominate the roads, reducing traffic accidents caused by human error and optimizing traffic flow. AI-powered public transportation systems ensure that buses, trains, and other modes of transport run on time and adapt to changing passenger needs. Electric and self-driving cars reduce emissions, contributing to a cleaner environment. AI also enables seamless integration of various transportation modes, allowing people to travel effortlessly from one place to another.

Education

Education in this utopian world is personalized and accessible to all. AI tutors provide individualized learning experiences, adapting to each student's strengths and weaknesses. Virtual classrooms powered by AI offer interactive and engaging lessons, making learning enjoyable and effective. AI systems analyze students' progress and provide real-time feedback, helping them achieve their full potential. Lifelong learning is encouraged, with AI offering personalized courses and resources to help individuals continuously develop their skills and knowledge.

Environmental Conservation

AI plays a crucial role in environmental conservation, helping to protect and preserve the planet. Advanced AI models predict climate patterns and develop strategies to mitigate the effects of climate change. AI-powered drones monitor wildlife populations and track endangered species, aiding in conservation efforts. Smart cities use AI to optimize energy consumption, reduce waste, and improve sustainability. AI also helps in managing natural resources, ensuring that they are used efficiently and responsibly.

Economy and Employment

In this utopian world, the economy thrives as AI drives innovation and productivity. AI automates routine and repetitive tasks, freeing up human workers to focus on creative and strategic roles. Job displacement is mitigated through comprehensive reskilling and upskilling programs, ensuring that workers can transition to new roles in the AI-driven economy. Income inequality is reduced as AI creates new opportunities and industries, distributing wealth more equitably. AI also enhances workplace safety, reducing the risk of accidents and injuries.

Social and Ethical Considerations

Ethical AI development is a cornerstone of this utopian society. AI systems are designed to be fair, transparent, and accountable, ensuring that they do not perpetuate biases or discrimination. Privacy is protected, with robust data protection measures in place to safeguard individuals' personal information. AI is used to promote social good, addressing issues such as poverty, inequality, and access to healthcare and education. Public awareness and education about AI ensure that society is informed and engaged in discussions about the technology's future.

Human-AI Collaboration

In this utopian world, humans and AI work together harmoniously. AI enhances human capabilities, providing tools and insights that help people make better decisions and solve complex problems. AI systems are designed to be user-friendly and intuitive, making them accessible to everyone. Human creativity and empathy are complemented by AI's analytical and computational power, leading to a society where technology and humanity coexist and thrive together.

In this utopian AI world, the best positive potential of AI is harnessed to create a society that is healthier, more sustainable, and more equitable. AI enhances every aspect of life, from healthcare and education to transportation and environmental conservation, fostering a harmonious and prosperous existence for all.

Dystopian AI World

In the dystopian AI world, the negative aspects of AI dominate, leading to a fragmented and unequal society. AI technologies exacerbate existing problems and create new challenges, resulting in a world where technology harms rather than helps humanity. Healthcare is plagued by biases and privacy violations, transportation is inefficient and unsafe, and education is characterized by a deepening digital divide. Job displacement and income inequality are rampant, and ethical considerations are ignored. AI-powered surveillance systems compromise privacy, and biases in AI algorithms lead to discrimination and unfair treatment. In this scenario, the unchecked development and deployment of AI technologies result in a society that is fraught with ethical and social issues.

Imagine a Dystopian AI world, where the best positive potential of AI has not been cultivated.

Imagine a world where artificial intelligence (AI) has not been harnessed for its positive potential, leading to a dystopian society where technology exacerbates existing problems and creates new challenges. In this dystopian AI world, the negative aspects of AI dominate, resulting in a society that is fragmented, unequal, and fraught with ethical and social issues.

Healthcare

In this dystopian world, AI in healthcare is plagued by biases and privacy violations. AI algorithms, trained on biased datasets, make inaccurate diagnoses and treatment recommendations, disproportionately affecting marginalized communities. Patients' personal health data is frequently breached and misused, leading to a loss of trust in the healthcare system. The lack of regulation and oversight allows for the proliferation of untested and unsafe AI-powered medical devices, putting patients' lives at risk.

Transportation

The transportation sector is dominated by autonomous vehicles that are poorly regulated and prone to malfunctions. Frequent accidents caused by AI-driven cars lead to a high number of fatalities and injuries. Traffic management systems, controlled by AI, are inefficient and fail to adapt to real-time conditions, resulting in chronic congestion and pollution. Public transportation systems are neglected, leaving many people without reliable and affordable means of travel.

Education

Education in this dystopian world is characterized by a deepening digital divide. AI-powered personalized learning platforms are only accessible to the wealthy, leaving disadvantaged students with outdated and inadequate educational resources. AI tutors, designed to replace human teachers, lack empathy and fail to address the diverse needs of students. The focus on standardized testing and data-driven metrics stifles creativity and critical thinking, producing a generation of students ill-prepared for the complexities of the real world.

Environmental Conservation

AI's potential to aid in environmental conservation is squandered in this dystopian world. AI-driven industrial processes prioritize profit over sustainability, leading to rampant pollution and resource depletion. Climate modeling and prediction systems are underfunded and inaccurate, hindering efforts to combat climate change. AI-powered surveillance technologies are used to exploit natural resources rather than protect them, resulting in the destruction of ecosystems and loss of biodiversity.

Economy and Employment

The economy is marked by extreme inequality, with AI-driven automation displacing millions of workers without providing adequate support for retraining and reskilling. The benefits of AI are concentrated in the hands of a few tech giants, exacerbating income inequality and creating a stark divide between the rich and the poor. Gig economy jobs, controlled by AI algorithms, offer little job security or benefits, leaving workers vulnerable and exploited.

Social and Ethical Considerations

Ethical considerations are largely ignored in this dystopian society. AI systems are opaque and unaccountable, making decisions that affect people's lives without transparency or recourse. Privacy is a thing of the past, with AI-powered surveillance systems monitoring every aspect of individuals' lives. Discrimination and bias are rampant, as AI algorithms perpetuate and amplify existing social inequalities. The lack of ethical guidelines and oversight leads to the development and deployment of AI technologies that harm rather than help society.

Human-AI Interaction

In this dystopian world, human-AI interaction is characterized by a lack of trust and understanding. AI systems are designed to replace rather than augment human capabilities, leading to a loss of jobs and skills. People become increasingly isolated and dependent on technology, losing the ability to think critically and solve problems independently. The human touch is lost in interactions with AI-powered customer service and healthcare systems, leading to a sense of alienation and disconnection.

In this dystopian AI world, the failure to harness the positive potential of AI results in a society that is fragmented, unequal, and fraught with ethical and social issues. The unchecked development and deployment of AI technologies exacerbate existing problems and create new challenges, leading to a world where technology harms rather than helps humanity.

Mediocre AI World

The mediocre AI world presents a mixed reality where AI has taken control of many aspects of life, but the results are neither entirely positive nor entirely negative. While AI provides efficiency and convenience, it also leads to a diminished human experience. Healthcare relies heavily on AI, but the lack of human touch leaves patients feeling isolated. Autonomous vehicles dominate transportation, but the joy of driving and spontaneity of travel are lost. Education is personalized by AI, but the absence of human teachers stifles creativity and critical thinking. Job displacement and economic inequality persist, and ethical considerations are often overlooked. In this world, AI's potential is not fully realized, and the human experience is diminished.

Imagine a Mediocre AI world, where everything is a strange mix of diminished human life.

In a mediocre AI world, life has become a peculiar blend of human existence and AI dominance. This world is neither a utopia nor a dystopia, but rather a strange mix where AI has taken control of many aspects of life, leading to a diminished human experience. Here's a detailed account of such a world:

Healthcare

In this mediocre AI world, healthcare is heavily reliant on AI, but the results are mixed. AI systems handle diagnostics and treatment plans, often providing accurate and efficient care. However, the human touch is missing. Patients feel like they are interacting with machines rather than compassionate healthcare providers. While AI can quickly analyze medical data and suggest treatments, it lacks the empathy and understanding that human doctors provide. This leads to a sense of isolation and dissatisfaction among patients, who miss the personal connection and reassurance that comes from human interaction.

Transportation

Transportation is dominated by AI-controlled autonomous vehicles. These vehicles are efficient and reduce traffic accidents, but they also create a sense of monotony and detachment. People no longer drive their own cars or make decisions about their routes. Instead, they are passive passengers in AI-driven vehicles. Public transportation is also controlled by AI, leading to optimized schedules and routes, but the lack of human drivers and conductors makes the experience impersonal and sterile. The joy of driving and the spontaneity of travel are lost in this AI-controlled world.

Education

Education is another area where AI has taken control, with mixed results. AI-powered personalized learning platforms provide tailored education experiences, but the absence of human teachers diminishes the quality of education. Students interact with AI tutors that lack the ability to inspire, motivate, and understand the emotional needs of learners. The focus on data-driven metrics and standardized testing stifles creativity and critical thinking. While students may achieve high scores, they miss out on the holistic development that comes from human mentorship and guidance.

Employment

In this world, AI has automated many jobs, leading to increased efficiency and productivity. However, this has also resulted in widespread job displacement and a sense of purposelessness among workers. Many people find themselves in low-skill, gig economy jobs controlled by AI algorithms, offering little job security or satisfaction. The human workforce is undervalued, and the sense of fulfillment that comes from meaningful work is diminished. While AI creates new opportunities, the lack of adequate reskilling and upskilling programs leaves many workers struggling to adapt.

Social and Ethical Considerations

Ethical considerations are often overlooked in this mediocre AI world. AI systems operate with a degree of opacity, making decisions that affect people's lives without transparency or accountability. Privacy is frequently compromised, with AI-powered surveillance systems monitoring individuals' activities. Biases in AI algorithms lead to unfair treatment and discrimination, exacerbating social inequalities. The lack of robust ethical guidelines and oversight results in AI technologies that sometimes harm rather than help society.

Human-AI Interaction

Human-AI interaction is characterized by a lack of trust and understanding. People rely heavily on AI for everyday tasks, leading to a decline in critical thinking and problem-solving skills. The human touch is lost in interactions with AI-powered customer service and healthcare systems, leading to a sense of alienation and disconnection. While AI provides convenience and efficiency, it also creates a world where human relationships and interactions are diminished.

Environmental Conservation

AI plays a role in environmental conservation, but the efforts are inconsistent. While AI helps optimize energy consumption and reduce waste in some areas, it also contributes to environmental degradation in others. The focus on profit-driven AI applications leads to the exploitation of natural resources, and the lack of comprehensive environmental policies results in a mixed impact on sustainability.

In this mediocre AI world, the potential of AI is not fully realized, and the human experience is diminished. AI controls many aspects of life, providing efficiency and convenience, but at the cost of personal connection, fulfillment, and ethical considerations. This world serves as a reminder of the importance of balancing technological advancements with human values and needs.

A call to action

The Future Outlook of AI, and its Potential Impact on Society

As we look towards the future, it is realistic to anticipate that we will find ourselves living in a society that resembles the Mediocre AI world. In this world, AI will have a significant presence in our daily lives, providing efficiency and convenience, but also presenting challenges and complexities that we must navigate. The integration of AI into various sectors will bring both benefits and drawbacks, creating a mixed reality where human experiences are both enhanced and diminished.

In healthcare, AI will improve diagnostics and treatment plans, but the lack of human touch may leave patients feeling isolated. Autonomous vehicles will dominate transportation, offering safety and efficiency, but the joy of driving and spontaneity of travel will be lost. Education will be personalized by AI, but the absence of human teachers may stifle creativity and critical thinking. Job displacement and economic inequality will persist, and ethical considerations will often be overlooked.

To positively benefit from the futuristic power of AI and super AI, it is crucial for each of us to be aware of the potential impacts and actively engage in shaping the future of AI.

Here are some steps we must take, as our call to action:

1. **Stay Informed**: Continuously educate ourselves about AI technologies, their applications, and their implications. By staying informed, we can make better decisions and advocate for responsible AI use.

2. **Advocate for Ethical AI**: Support policies and initiatives that promote fairness, accountability, and transparency in AI development. Advocate for regulations that protect privacy and ensure the responsible use of AI.

3. **Promote Inclusivity**: Encourage the involvement of diverse stakeholders in AI development, including

ethicists, sociologists, and representatives from affected communities. This will help create AI systems that are more inclusive and equitable.

4. **Foster Education and Public Awareness**: Support educational programs that teach AI literacy and critical thinking skills. Promote public awareness campaigns that highlight both the benefits and risks of AI, fostering a balanced and informed understanding of the technology.

5. **Engage in Ethical Practices**: If you are involved in AI development or deployment, prioritize ethical considerations in your work. Strive to create AI systems that are free from bias, respect privacy, and enhance human well-being.

By taking these steps, we can collectively harness the positive potential of AI while addressing its challenges. In doing so, we can ensure that AI serves as a force for good, driving progress and improving the quality of life for all. The future of AI is in our hands, and it is up to us to shape it in a way that benefits humanity.

The AI revolution is a double-edged sword, offering both tremendous opportunities and significant risks. By carefully balancing these aspects, we can shape a future where AI serves as a force for positive change, driving progress and improving the well-being of humanity.

Epilogue

As we reach the end of this journey through the transformative world of Artificial Intelligence, it is clear that AI holds immense potential to revolutionize our lives. From healthcare and transportation to education and environmental conservation, AI is already making significant strides in various sectors. However, with great power comes great responsibility. It is crucial to navigate the benefits and risks of AI thoughtfully and ethically.

The future of AI is in the hands of the young people and future generations who will be the torchbearers of this technology. Their curiosity, creativity, and passion will drive the innovations that will shape our future. It is up to us to ensure that they are equipped with the knowledge and tools to harness AI's potential for the greater good.

As we move forward, let us remember the lessons learned and the challenges faced. Let us strive to create a future where AI serves as a force for good, driving progress and improving the quality of life for all. Together, we can build a brighter, more inclusive, and sustainable world.

Thank you for joining me on this exploration of AI. May this book inspire you to continue learning, questioning, and innovating in the ever-evolving field of Artificial Intelligence.

Synopsis

Throughout this book, we have explored the multifaceted nature of artificial intelligence (AI) and its profound impact on various aspects of our lives. We began with a historical overview of AI development, tracing its roots from early theoretical concepts to the advanced technologies we see today. We highlighted key milestones and breakthroughs that have shaped the field, such as the development of expert systems, machine learning, and deep learning.

We then delved into the positive aspects of AI, showcasing its potential to revolutionize industries such as healthcare, transportation, education, and environmental conservation. AI's ability to enhance diagnostics, personalize medicine, improve traffic management, enable personalized learning, and aid in wildlife protection demonstrates its immense potential to benefit society.

However, we also examined the not-so-good aspects of AI, depending on how we will continue to navigate the complexities of AI power, addressing ethical concerns like bias in algorithms and privacy issues, economic impacts such as job displacement and income inequality, security risks including AI in cyber warfare and autonomous weapons, and social implications like dependency on technology and the loss of human touch.

We also discussed strategies for balancing the benefits and risks of AI. This includes ethical AI development practices, robust policies and regulations, and the importance of education and public awareness in shaping AI's future.

AI for All: Transformative Artificial Intelligence

About the Author

Dr. Farzana Chohan is a visionary founder of Optimize Excellence, an organization dedicated to developing innovative workplace solutions. With a distinguished career as a speaker for Fortune 500 companies and TEDx, Dr. Chohan addresses vital subjects such as Leadership, Artificial Intelligence, Belonging Work Culture, and Human Excellence. Renowned for her expertise in cultivating Human Excellence, she plays an essential role in promoting professional development and success.

Dr. Chohan's platform, Optimize Excellence, helps organizations encourage continuous improvement and foster a sense of community. As a leadership mentor, she guides organizations through obstacles, helping them realize their utmost potential. Her commitment to human excellence is evident in her work, where she emphasizes the importance of ethical leadership, inclusive work cultures, and continuous personal and professional growth.

With AI on the brink of significantly shaping the future of human excellence and its influence on life, Dr. Farzana

Chohan is dedicated to the constructive integration of AI. She ensures its ethical application and strives to enhance human existence and excellence through technology. Her insights and expertise make her an invaluable resource for understanding the transformative impact of AI on our world.

In this book "AI for All," Dr. Chohan brings her extensive knowledge and experience to the forefront. This book provides a comprehensive exploration of AI, highlighting both its promises and perils. Through real-world examples and practical insights, Dr. Chohan offers a balanced view of AI, acknowledging its potential benefits while addressing the challenges and risks associated with its development and integration into society.

Whether you're a tech enthusiast, a business leader, or simply curious about the future of AI, Dr. Chohan's book will equip you with the knowledge to navigate the AI landscape and harness its transformative power for good. Join her on this enlightening journey and discover how we can collectively shape a future where AI serves as a force for positive change, driving progress and improving the quality of life for all.

AI for All: Transformative Artificial Intelligence

AI for All: Transformative Artificial Intelligence

AI for All: Transformative Artificial Intelligence

83

AI for All: Transformative Artificial Intelligence